DENISE LEVERTOV

With
eyes
at the
back
of our
heads

A NEW DIRECTIONS BOOK

New Directions Books are published by James Laughlin at Norfolk, Connecticut

New York Office — 333 Sixth Avenue (14)

FOR

MITCHELL AND

NIKOLAI GOODMAN

CONTENTS

WITH
EYES
AT THE
BACK
OF OUR
HEADS

• THE ARTIST

(From the Spanish translation of Toltec Códice de la Real Academia, fol. 315, v. *With the help of Elvira Abascal who understood the original Toltec.)*

The artist: disciple, abundant, multiple, restless.
The true artist: capable, practicing, skillful;
maintains dialogue with his heart, meets things with his mind.

The true artist: draws out all from his heart,
works with delight, makes things with calm, with sagacity,
works like a true Toltec, composes his objects, works dexterously, invents;
arranges materials, adorns them, makes them adjust.

The carrion artist: works at random, sneers at the people,
makes things opaque, brushes across the surface of the face of things,
works without care, defrauds people, is a thief.

4

• EL ARTISTA

El artista: discípulo, abundante, múltiple, inquieto.
El verdadero artista: capaz, se adiestra, es hábil;
dialoga con su corazón, encuentra las cosas con su mente.

El verdadero artista todo lo saca de su corazón,
obra con deleite, hace las cosas con calma, con tiento,
obra como un tolteca, compone cosas, obra hábilmente, crea;
arregla las cosas, las hace atildadas, hace que se ajusten.

El torpe artista: obra al azar, se burla de la gente,
opaca las cosas, pasa por encima del rostro de la cosas,
obra sin cuidado, defrauda a las personas, es un ladrón.

• TOLTECATL

In toltecatl; tlamachtilli, tolih, centozon, aman.
In qualli toltecatl: mozcaliani, mozcaliz, mihmati;
moyolnonotzani, tlalnamiquini.

In qualli toltecatl tlayollocopaviani,
tlapaccachivani, tlaiviyanchivani, tlamavhcachiva,
toltecati, tlatalia, tlahimati, tlayocoya; —
tlavipana, tlapopotia, tlananamictia.

In xolopihtli toltecatl; tlailivizviani, teca mocayavani,
tlaixpachoani, iixco quihquiza,
tlailivizvia, teca mocayava, ichtequi.

5

WITH

EYES

AT THE

BACK

OF OUR

HEADS

• WITH EYES AT THE BACK OF OUR HEADS

With eyes at the back of our heads
we see a mountain
not obstructed with woods but laced
here and there with feathery groves.

The doors before us in a facade
that perhaps has no house in back of it
are too narrow, and one is set high
with no doorsill. The architect sees

the imperfect proposition and
turns eagerly to the knitter.
Set it to rights!
The knitter begins to knit.

For we want
to enter the house, if there is a house,
to pass through the doors at least
into whatever lies beyond them,

we want to enter the arms
of the knitted garment. As one
is re-formed, so the other,
in proportion.

When the doors widen
when the sleeves admit us
the way to the mountain will clear,

9

the mountain we see with
eyes at the back of our heads, mountain
green, mountain
cut of limestone, echoing
with hidden rivers, mountain
of short grass and subtle shadows.

• THE CHARGE

Returning

    to all the unsaid
all the lost living untranslated
in any sense,
and the dead
unrecognized, celebrated
only in dreams that die by morning

is a mourning or ghostwalking only.
    You must make, said music

    in its voices of metal and wood
in its dancing diagrams, moving
apart and together, along
    and over and under a line
and speaking in one voice,

        make
my image.   Let be
what is gone.

• THE DEPARTURE

Have you got the moon safe?
Please, tie those strings a little tighter.
This loaf, push it down further
the light is crushing it — such a baguette
golden brown and so white inside
you don't see every day
nowadays. And for God's sake
don't let's leave in the end
without the ocean! Put it
in there among the shoes, and
tie the moon on behind. It's time!

● THE FIVE-DAY RAIN

The washing hanging from the lemon tree
in the rain
and the grass long and coarse.

Sequence broken, tension
of sunlight broken.
                              So light a rain

fine shreds
pending above the rigid leaves.

Wear scarlet! Tear the green lemons
off the tree!   I don't want
to forget who I am, what has burned in me
and hang limp and clean, an empty dress —

13

• THE DEAD BUTTERFLY

I

Now I see its whiteness
is not white but green, traced with green,
and resembles the stones
of which the city is built,
quarried high in the mountains.

II

Everywhere among the marigolds
the rainblown roses and the hedges
of tamarisk are white
butterflies this morning, in constant
tremulous movement, only those
that lie dead revealing
their rockgreen color and the bold
cut of the wings.

• THE LOST BLACK-AND-WHITE CAT

Cockcrowing at midnight.   Broken
silence. Crickets skillfully re-
forming it in
                minims and
quavers.   The child turns, bangs
     the headboard, struggles
with dreams. Last night in dreams
he found the cat in the bathroom.

             Come back, cat.
Thrash the silence with your autonomous
feather tail. Imagination made fur,
come back, spring poems out of the whole
cloth of silence.

• THE LAGOON

This lagoon with its glass shadows
and naked golden shallows
the mangrove island, home of white herons,

recalls the Loire at La Charité
that ran swiftly in quiet ripples
brimful of clouds from the evening sky.

In both, the presence of a rippling quiet
        limpid over the sandbars, suspended,
        and drawing over the depths
long lines of beveled darkness,
draws the mind
down to its own depths

where the imagination swims,
shining dark-scaled fish,
swims and waits, flashes, waits and
wavers, shining of its own light.

• PLEASURES

I like to find
what's not found
at once, but lies

within something of another nature,
in repose, distinct.
Gull feathers of glass, hidden

in white pulp: the bones of squid
which I pull out and lay
blade by blade on the draining board —

     tapered as if for swiftness, to pierce
     the heart, but fragile, substance
     belying design.   Or a fruit, *mamey*,

cased in rough brown peel, the flesh
rose-amber, and the seed:
the seed a stone of wood, carved and

polished, walnut-colored, formed
like a brazilnut, but large,
large enough to fill
the hungry palm of a hand.

I like the juicy stem of grass that grows
within the coarser leaf folded round,
and the butteryellow glow

17

in the narrow flute from which the morning-glory
opens blue and cool on a hot morning.

• THE OFFENDER

The eye luminous
in its box of ebony
saw the point of departure, a room
pleasant, bare, sunlit,
and space beyond it, time
extending to mountains, ending,
beginning new space beyond.

The eye, luminous, grayblue,
a moonstone,
brimmed over with mercury tears
that rolled and were lost in sunny dust.
The world in the lustre of a
black pupil moved its clouds
and their shadows. Time
had gathered itself and gone. The eye
luminous, prince of solitude.

• SEEMS LIKE WE MUST BE SOMEWHERE ELSE

Sweet procession, rose-blue,
and all them bells.

Bandstand red, the eyes
at treetop level seeing it. "Are we
what we think we are or are we
what befalls us?"

The people from an open window
the eyes
seeing it!   Daytime!   Or twilight!

Sweet procession, rose-blue.
If we're here let's be here now.

And the train whistle? who
invented that? Lonesome man, wanted the trains
to speak for him.

19

• OBSESSIONS

Maybe it is true we have to return
to the black air of ashcan city
because it is there the most life was burned,

as ghosts or criminals return?
But no, the city has no monopoly
of intense life. The dust burned

golden or violet in the wide land
to which we ran away, images
of passion sprang out of the land

as whirlwinds or red flowers, your hands
opened in anguish or clenched in violence
under that sun, and clasped my hands

in that place to which we will not return
where so much happened that no one else noticed,
where the city's ashes that we brought with us
flew into the intense sky still burning.

• TRIPLE FEATURE

Innocent decision: to enjoy.
And the pathos
of hopefulness, of his solicitude:

— he in mended serape,
she having plaited carefully
magenta ribbons into her hair,
the baby a round half-hidden shape
slung in her rebozo, and the young son steadfastly
gripping a fold of her skirt,
pale and severe under a
handed-down sombrero —

        all regarding
the stills with full attention, preparing
to pay and go in —
to worlds of shadow-violence, half-
familiar, warm with popcorn, icy
with strange motives, barbarous splendors!

• A LETTER

I know you will come, bringing me
an opal. Good! I will come
to meet you. And walk back with you
to meet whatever it is raves to us
for release.   New courage
has stirred in me while you were gone.
They are stripping the bark from the trees
to make soup
and sitting down I crush fifty
blackeyed susans, each no bigger than a
one-cent piece.   I'm tired
of all that is not mine. Lighting
two cigarettes by mistake, lying back
one in each hand, surprised,
Buddha of the anthill. A great day!
The first to waken as a bear
from cosy smelly comfort ("a rock
dressed in brown moss, little eyes
glinting") and walk out
to the hunt.

• ANOTHER JOURNEY

From a world composed, closed to us,
back to nowhere, the north.
                              We need
a cold primrose sting
of east wind; we need
a harsh design of magic lights at night over
drab streets, tears
salting our mouths, whether the east wind
brought them or the jabbing
of memories and perceptions, who knows.
            Not history, but our own histories,
a brutal dream drenched with our lives,
intemperate, open, illusory,

     to which we wake, sweating to make
substance of it, grip it, turn
its face to us, unwilling, and see the
snowflakes glitter there, and melt.

• THE TAKE OFF

The mountains through the shadowy
flickering of the propellers, steady,
melancholy, relaxed, indifferent, a world
lost to our farewells.
                         The rising of the smoke
from valleys, the pearly waters, the
tight-lipped brown fields, all is relaxed,
melancholy, steady, radiant with dawn stillness,
the world indivisible, from which we fly —
sparks, motes, flickers
of energy, willful, afraid, uttering
harsh interior cries, silent, waving and smiling to the
invisible guardians of our losses.

• GIRLHOOD OF JANE HARRISON

At a window —
so much is easy to see:

an outleaning from indoor darkness
to garden darkness.

But marzipan! Could so much sweetness
not seem banal?

No: it was a calling of
roses by other names.

Now from, as it may be,
the cedar tree

out went the points of the star.
The dance was a stamping in

of autumn. A dance in the garden
to welcome the fall. The diagram

was a diamond, like the pan
for star-cake.   Multiplied,

the dancer moved outward to all the
promontories of shadow, the

forest bays, the moon islands. With
roses of marzipan
the garden dissolved its boundaries.

25

• A HAPPENING

Two birds, flying East, hit the night
at three in the afternoon; stars came out
over the badlands and the billowy
snowlands; they floundered on
resolving not to turn back in search
of lost afternoon; continuing
through cotton wildernesses
through the stretched night
and caught up with dawn in a rainstorm
in the city, where they fell
in semblance of torn paper sacks
to the sidewalk on 42nd St., and resumed
their human shape, and separated:
one turned uptown, to follow
the Broadway river to its possible source,
the other downtown, to see
the fair and goodly harbor; but each,
accosted by shadows that muttered to him
pleading mysteriously, half-hostile, was drawn
into crosstown streets, into
revolving doorways, into nameless
small spaces back of buildings,
airless airshafts, till no more
was known of man, bird, nor paper.

• THE VIGIL

When the mice awaken
and come out to their work of searching
for life, crumbs of life,
I sit quiet in my back room
trying to quiet my mind of its chattering,
rumors and events, and find
life, crumbs of life, to nourish it
until in stillness, replenished,
the animal god within the
cluttered shrine   speaks.   Alas!
poor mice — I have left
nothing for them, no bread,
no fat, not an unwashed plate.
Go through the walls to other kitchens;
let it be silent here.
I'll sit in vigil
awaiting the Cat
who with human tongue
speaks inhuman oracles
or delicately, with its claws, opens
Chinese boxes, each containing
the World and its shadow.

• THE ROOM

With a mirror
I could see the sky.

With two mirrors or three
justly placed, I could see
the sun bowing to the evening chimneys.

Moonrise — the moon itself might appear
in a fourth mirror placed high
and close to the open window.

           With enough mirrors within
and even without the room, a cantilever
supporting them, mountains
and oceans might be manifest.

I understand perfectly
that I could encounter my own eyes
too often — I take account
of the danger — .
           If the mirrors
are large enough, and arranged
with bravura, I can look
beyond my own glance.

With one mirror
how many stars could I see?

I don't want to escape, only to see
the enactment of rites.

28

• THE SAGE

The cat is eating the roses:
that's the way he is.
Don't stop him, don't stop
the world going round,
that's the way things are.
The third of May
was misty; fourth of May
who knows. Sweep
the rose-meat up, throw the bits
out in the rain.
He never eats
every crumb, says
the hearts are bitter.
That's the way he is, he knows
the world and the weather.

• THE COMMUNION

A pondering frog looks
out from my eyes:

dark-red, veiled blue, plums
roll to the center of a bowl

and at close horizon water-towers
hump and perch.

              Leap
frog, to a lake: leaves
support the lilies, water holds

erect the long, strong stems,
reflects gleaming

rosy petals, pollen-yellow lily-buds,
clouds lilac-tinted and dissolving.
Back to the plums —

eggs in a blue nest — the squat
peaked assembly of towers.

What is it?
             An accord.

Break out, frog,
sing, you who don't know

anything about anything.
"To dance without moving" shall be your burden.

30

• FEBRUARY EVENING IN NEW YORK

As the stores close, a winter light
   opens air to iris blue,
   glint of frost through the smoke,
   grains of mica, salt of the sidewalk.
As the buildings close, released autonomous
   feet pattern the streets
   in hurry and stroll; balloon heads
   drift and dive above them; the bodies
   aren't really there.
As the lights brighten, as the sky darkens,
   a woman with crooked heels says to another woman
   while they step along at a fair pace,
   "You know, I'm telling you, what I love best
   is life. I love life! Even if I ever get
   to be old and wheezy — or limp! You know?
   Limping along? — I'd still . . ." Out of hearing.
To the multiple disordered tones
   of gears changing, a dance
   to the compass points, out, four-way river.
   Prospect of sky
   wedged into avenues, left at the ends of streets,
   west sky, east sky: more life tonight! A range
   of open time at winter's outskirts.

• A STRAW SWAN UNDER THE CHRISTMAS TREE

Its form speaks of gliding
  though one had never seen a swan

  and strands of silver, caught
  in the branches near it, speak

of rain suspended in a beam of light,

  one speech conjuring the other.

  All trivial parts of
  world-about-us speak in their forms
  of themselves and their counterparts!

Rain glides aslant,
  swan pauses in mid-stroke,
   stamped on the mind's light, but aloof —

and the eye that sees them refuses
to see further, glances off the
surfaces that
    speak and conjure,
rests

  on the frail
  strawness of straw, metal sheen of tinsel.

  How far might one go
  treading the cleft the swan cut?

32

• THE DEAD

Earnestly I looked
into their abandoned faces
at the moment of death and while
I bandaged their slack jaws and
straightened waxy unresistant limbs and plugged
the orifices with cotton
but like everyone else I learned
each time nothing new, only that
as it were, a music, however harsh, that held us
however loosely, had stopped, and left
a heavy thick silence in its place.

33

• NOTES OF A SCALE

I

A noon with twilight overtones
from open windows looking down.
Hell! it goes by. The trees
practice green in faithful measure.
It could be what I'm waiting for is
not here at all. Yet
the trees have it, don't they?
Absorbed in their own magic,
abundant, hermetic, wide open.

II

The painting within itself,
a boy that has learned to whistle,
a fisherman. The painting
living its magic, admitting
nothing, being, the boy
pushing his hands further into his
pockets, the fisherman
beginning the day, in dew and half-dark,
by a river whose darkness
will be defined as brown in a
half-hour. The painting
suspended in itself, an angler
in the suspense of daybreak,
whistling to itself.

34

III

Where the noon passes
in camouflage of twilight

doesn't cease to look
into it from his oblique
angle, leafwise,
"...maintains dialog with his heart,"

doesn't spill the beans
balances like a papaya tree on a single
young elephant-leg.

IV

A glass brimming, not spilling,
the green trees
practising their art.
                    'A wonder
    from the true world,'
he who accomplished it
            'overwhelmed with the wonder
which rises out of his doing.'

Note: See 'The True Wonder,' anecdote of Rabbi
Elimélekh of Lijensk in Buber's *Tales of the Hasidim:
The Early Masters*

• TERROR

Face-down; odor
of dusty carpet. The grip
of anguished stillness.

Then your naked voice, your
head knocking the wall, sideways,
the beating of trapped thoughts against iron.

If I remember, how is it
my face shows
barely a line? Am I
a monster, to sing
in the wind on this sunny hill

and not taste the dust always,
and not hear
that rending, that retching?
How did morning come, and the days
that followed, and quiet nights?

• A RING OF CHANGES

I

Shells, husks, the wandering
of autumn seeds, the loitering
of curled indoor leaves holding
by a cobweb to the bark
many days before falling.

Cracking husk, afraid
it may reveal a dirty emptiness
afraid its hazelnut may be green,
bitter, of no account.

.   .   .   .

Seed, cling
to the hard earth, some footstep
will grind you in,

new leaf, open your green hand,
old leaf, fall and rot
enriching your rich brotherhood,

hazelnut, know when ripeness
has hardened you and sweetened you.

II

To shed this fake face
as a snakeskin, paper

37

dragon the winds will tear —
to dig shame up, a buried bone
and tie it to my breast —

(would it change, in time,
to an ornament? Could it serve
to be carved with new designs?)

III

I look among your papers
for something that will give you to me
until you come back;
and find: *"Where are my dreams?"*

Your dreams! Have they not nourished my life?
Didn't I poach among them, as now on your desk?
My cheeks grown red and my hair curly
as I roasted your pheasants by my night fire!
    My dreams are gone off to hunt yours,
I won't take them back unless they find yours,
they must return torn by your forests.

Unremembered
               our dreams move together
in our dark heads, wander
in landscapes unlit by our candle eyes
eyes of self love and self disgust
eyes of your love for me kindling my cold heart
eyes of my love for you flickering at the edge of you.

38

IV

Among the tall elders of the hereafter
my father had become
                    a blissful foolish rose
his face beaming from among petals
(of sunset pink) 'open as a daisy' —
a rose walking, tagging at the heels
of the wise, having found
a true form.

V

The tree of life is growing
in a corner of the living-room
held to its beam by nails
that encircle, not pierce, its stem.
From its first shoots, many leaves,
then a long, curved, and back-curving bare stretch,
and above, many leaves, many new shoots,
spreading left along the wall, and right,
towards your worktables.

Casals' cello (a live broadcast: the resistances
            of the live bow, the passion manifest
            in living hands, not smoothed out on wax)
speaks from across the room
and the tree of life answers
with its green silence and apparent stillness.

The cello is hollow and the stems are hollow.
The space of the cello is shaped; no other form would resound
with the same tones; the stems at their branchings-off
widen, and narrow to a new growth.
As bow touches strings, a voice is heard;
at the articulations of green, a path
moves toward a leaf. There is space in us

but the lines and planes of its form
are what we reach for and fall,
touching nothing (outside ourselves and yet
                    standing somewhere within our own space,
                    in its darkness).
Buds are knots in our flesh, nodules of pain.

What holds us upright, once we have faced
immeasurable darkness, the black point
at our eyes' center? Were we suspended,
museum butterflies, by a filament, from a hidden nail?
Has it broken when we begin to
fall, slowly, without desire?
(But we don't fall. The floor is flat, the round earth
is flat, and we stand on it, and though we lie down
and fill our lungs with choking dust
and spread our arms to make a cross
after a while we rise and creep away,
walk from one room to another
'on our feet again.')

40

Your worktable
is close to the tree — not a tree perhaps,
a vine.
In time the leaves
will reach the space above it, between the windows.

Cello and vine commune
in the space of a room.

What will speak to you?
What notes of abundance
strike across the living room
to your bowed head and down-curved back?

Watch the beloved vine. We can't
see it move.

Listen, listen . . .
We are in this room
together. You are alone
forming darkness into words
dark on white paper,
I am alone with the sense of your anguish.
The tree of life is growing in the room,
the living-room, the work-room.

VI

Between the white louvers, nectarine
light, and on the carpet's earthbrown, amber,
entered, filled unpeopled space with presence.

From the doorway we saw
harmonies and heard
measured colors of light, not quite awake and so awake
to correspondences. A room in a house in the city
became for a space of fine, finely-drawn,
November morning, a Holy Apple Field.

And from the table to the crimson
blanket, from the other, carved, table
to the ashes of last night's fire, slanted
louvered light, passing without haste.
We watched from the doorway between sleeping and waking.
Green to the white ceiling drew the vine.

• THE GODDESS

She in whose lipservice
I passed my time,
whose name I knew, but not her face,
came upon me where I lay in Lie Castle!

Flung me across the room, and
room after room (hitting the walls, re-
bounding — to the last
sticky wall — wrenching away from it
pulled hair out!)
till I lay
outside the outer walls!

There in cold air
lying still where her hand had thrown me,
I tasted the mud that splattered my lips:
the seeds of a forest were in it,
asleep and growing! I tasted
her power!

The silence was answering my silence,
a forest was pushing itself
out of sleep between my submerged fingers.

I bit on a seed and it spoke on my tongue
of day that shone already among stars
in the water-mirror of low ground,

43

and a wind rising ruffled the lights:
she passed near me returning from the encounter,
she who plucked me from the close rooms,

without whom nothing
flowers, fruits, sleeps in season,
without whom nothing
speaks in its own tongue, but returns
lie for lie!

• UNDER THE TREE

Under an orange-tree —
not one especial singular
orange-tree, but one among

the dark multitude. Recline
there, with a stone winejar

and the sense
of another dream
concentration would capture —
but it doesn't matter —

and the sense
of dust on the grass, of infinitesimal
flowers, of
cracks in the earth

and urgent life
passing there, ants and transparent
winged beings in their intensity
traveling from blade to blade,

under a modest orange-tree
neither lower nor taller
neither darker-leaved nor aglow
more beneficently

45

than the dark multitude
glowing in numberless lanes
the orange-farmer counts, but
not you — recline

and drink wine — the stone
will keep it cold — with the sense
of life yet to be lived — rest, rest,
the grass is growing —

let the oranges
ripen, ripen above you,
you are living too, one
among the dark multitude —

• FRITILLARY

A chequered lily,
fritillary, named
for a dicebox, shall be
our emblem

and the butterfly
so like it one would see
a loose petal blowing
if it flew over
                where the flowers grew.

A field flower
but rare,
chequered dark and light,

and its winged semblance
lapsing from sky to earth,

fritillary, a chance word
speaking of glancing shadows, of
flying fluttering delights, to be

our talisman in sorrow.

47

• THE WIFE

A frog under you,
knees drawn up
ready to leap out of time,

a dog beside you,
snuffing at you, seeking
scent of you, an idea unformulated,

I give up on
trying to answer my question,
Do I love you enough?

It's enough to be
so much here. And
certainly when I catch

your mind in the
act of plucking
truth from the dark surrounding nowhere

as a swallow skims a
gnat from the
deep sky,

I don't stop to ask myself
Do I love him? but
laugh for joy.

48

• AT THE EDGE

How much I should like to begin
a poem with And — presupposing
the hardest said —
the moss cleared off the stone,
the letters plain.
How the round moon
would shine into all the corners
of such a poem and show
the words! Moths and dazzled
awakened birds
would freeze in its light!
The lines would be
an outbreak of bells
and I swinging on the rope!

Yet, not desiring apocrypha
but true revelation,
what use to pretend the stone discovered,
anything visible?
That poem indeed
may not be carved there, may lie
— the quick of mystery —
in animal eyes gazing
from the thicket,
a creature of unknown size,
fierce, terrified, having teeth or
no defense, but whom
no And may approach suddenly.

49

• AN IGNORANT PERSON

Way out there where words jump
in the haze
is the land of hot mamas.

Or say, in the potato patch
a million bugs glittering green and bronze
climb up and down the stems
exchanging perceptions.

                I in my balloon
light where the wind
permits a landing,
in my own province.

• THE GREAT DAHLIA

Great lion-flower, whose flames
are tipped with white,
so it seems each petal's fire
burns out in snowy ash,

a dawn bird will light
on the kitchen table
to sing at midday for you

and have you noticed?
a green spider came with you
from the garden where they cut you,
to be the priest of your temple.

Burn, burn the day. The wind
is trying to enter and praise you.
Silence seems something you have chosen,
withholding your bronze voice.
We bow before your pride.

• BREAD

As florid berries to the oak, should I pin
sequins to this Rockland County bouquet
of bare twigs? — as roses
to pineboughs? — While a primrose-yellow
apple, flushed with success, levitates quietly
in the top right-hand corner of a small canvas,
giving pleasure by its happiness?
But these are thin pleasures, to content
the contented. For hunger:
the bare stretching thorny branches that may never speak
though they conceal or half-reveal
sharp small syllables of bud; and the ragged laughter
— showing gaps between its teeth —
of the anonymous weeds, towsle-heads,
yellow-brown like the draggled undersides of
dromedary and llama basking
proud and complete in airy wedges
of April sun — something
of endurance, to endure
ripeness if it come, or suffer
a slow spring with lifted head —
a good crust of brown bread for the hungry.

• THE DOG OF ART

That dog with daisies for eyes
who flashes forth
flame of his very self at every bark
is the Dog of Art.
Worked in wool, his blind eyes
look inward to caverns and jewels
which they see perfectly,
and his voice
measures forth the treasure
in music sharp and loud,
sharp and bright,
bright flaming barks,
and growling smoky soft, the Dog
of Art turns to the world
the quietness of his eyes.

• A DREAM

A story was told me of the sea, of time suspended as calm seas balance and hover, of a breaking and hastening of time in sea tempest, of slow oil-heavy time turning its engines over in a sultry night at sea. The story belonged not to time but to the sea; its time and its men were of the sea, the sea held them, and the sea itself was bounded by darkness.

The man who told it was young when it began — a young ship's officer on that ship whose name he did not tell.

Among the crew — many of whom had sailed together many times before the young officer joined them — were two, Antonio and Sabrinus, who were regarded by the rest with a peculiar respectful affection.

These two were friends; and in the harmony of their responses, their communing quietness, seemed twin brothers, more than friends.

Their friendship, while it enclosed

them in its ring, did not arouse jealousy or contempt; a gentle and serene light glowed out from it and was seen as something fair and inviolable.

The Captain himself (rarely seen on deck) allowed them a special privilege: In an idle time Antonio had built with matchless skill a small boat of his own, which when completed he and Sabrinus painted a glowing red, not scarlet but bright carmine. This — slight and elegant as a shelf model, but fully seaworthy — Antonio was permitted to keep in special davits; and when the ship anchored in roads or harbor, or lay becalmed in midvoyage, he and Sabrinus would go fishing in her — sailing if there were wind enough, or rowing at times of glassy lull.

Even this caused no resentment. That they seemed to share thoughts as well as words — not many of the men understood their language, which may have been Portuguese or Catalan, or some island dialect — and that the catboat or skiff held only two, was tacitly accepted. An unfailing gentleness and kindly composure compensated for their reserve.

As for daily work, the ship's life, Antonio and Sabrinus were quick, sagacious, and diligent.

Indeed the young man soon came to realize that a belief had grown among the men that Antonio and Sabrinus were luck-bringers and that no evil would come to them or to the ship as long as those two were there.

So that when one night (or it may have begun on a dark day) a storm came up that grew fiercer hour by hour, it appeared to them at first 'only' a storm. The wind became a thing, solid, heavily insistent, lacking only visibility — and yet remained only the wind; and the spiring waves it whipped up, though they rose higher than the ship itself, and seemed about to devour everything they could reach, were still only waves; and confident that ship and voyage were under the protection of a special providence, manifested in the incandescent companionship of the holy friends, the crew staggered and

56

gripped and moved as they could about the lunging decks without true fear.

But there was an end to this time of brave activity; for as life slid violently aside and back, and the storm achieved its very orgasm, a chill silent fear struck the men, at seeing Antonio and Sabrinus in a new aspect — hatred marking their faces and bitter words breaking out between them. The cause of the quarrel was the crimson boat. Antonio, believing the ship about to sink, determined to loose and launch his artifact, and counted on his friend to take his chance of life in her with him, frail though she was in such a sea. But it seemed less the chance of life he desired than to give his boat her freedom, so that if she were destroyed it would be in open combat with the great ocean, not as a prisoner bound fast to the body of the ship. And Sabrinus refused.

Though the greater number of the listening men surrounding them on three sides (on the fourth was the sea itself) could not understand their lan-

57

guage, and those who did could catch only a few words from the storm's clamor, all understood that Sabrinus was saying, No, they must always as before stand by the ship to which they were committed, and help their fellows save her if they could — must share the common fate as if they were common men. Neither would be swayed by the other, and in a moment the two men, set apart in hatred as in love, set upon one another, oblivious of all that encircled them, in a murderous fight. As the young officer saw it, this hatred was the long-secreted flower of their love, the unsuspected fearful harvest of long calm voyages, of benevolent quietness and exclusive understandings.

Not a man but clung to whatever rail or stanchion he could find on the steep decks to see this abominable flowering, cold at heart. But no-one thought for a moment of stepping between them, it was the storm itself intervened: as Antonio and Sabrinus held one another in choking grip, the vessel was lifted in the sea's gleaming teeth. The deck shuddered and pitched them overboard into a great trough of the waters, as if to appease the great mouth.

Then the wind was no longer a thing, but an evil, multiple, personage; and the waves swept up upon them with intent of malice. The blessed cord that bound ship and men to happy fortune had broken. No-one listened to what orders they could hear, the Captain vanished from the bridge, and in half an hour the ship had split and sunk. The survivors, reaching shore, dispersed, and of them the story teller had no more to say.

But the story of Antonio and Sabrinus was not ended. This is what he told:

Many years later it happened that he found himself without a berth in an obscure, sleazy tropical port — perhaps in Central America, at all events in a hot, moist climate. Eager to get away from the sultry city, he shipped as first mate on the freighter *Jacobi* at very short notice, the officer he replaced having been taken seriously ill. The owners, only eager for the perishable cargo to reach its destination by a certain date, concealed from him the fact that there was fever aboard.

He joined the ship at dusk; by midnight they were well out to sea, and having soon become aware of the crew's depletion, he was musing angrily at the deception practiced on him, which the captain had shiftily admitted once they were out of port. A little after midnight he descended into the sick men's quarters.

The steaming darkness here was in sharp contrast to the bright moonlight he had just left. Dim lights swung here and there; crowded with hammocks and cramped bunks, the space in which these men were isolated seemed a hellish writhing mass of discolored and tormented forms.

He passed from one to another grimly inspecting the disorder, flashing a shielded light now on faces wild with delirium, now on swollen unmoving bodies, perhaps already dead. Nor was the horror all to the eyes; piercing cries and deep groans rose from this multitude into the sweating air in a unison to which the engines played ground-bass.

At length, in the furthest corner, he came to two men whose faces made him start; he bent to examine them more closely. The serenely joyful days of the long-ago voyage returned to his mind; Antonio and Sabrinus in all their luck-bringing radiance; and the fearful term of it, their flight, their plunge to death. But had they somehow swum to safety? Was it possible that they had after all been rescued? For here they lay — they or their doubles?

Long he looked — turned away — looked again. The features were the same; yet the faces looked darker. And the torn clothing on their thin bodies was of a kind traditional to one of the Malay Islands. Moreover the language in which, unconscious of him, they muttered in their fever, was not the Mediterranean tongue of Antonio and Sabrinus. But they lay, in their hammocks, so close to one another — a ring of difference invisibly separating them from the mass of men, as it had sepa-

61

rated Antonio and Sabrinus. Could it be that, rescued unimaginably from the storm, they had landed together on some island and in amnesia, or from mysterious will to obliterate all that had been, made its language their own? What of their hatred? If they had lived, then, had it passed, had they resumed their calm affection?

Or were they without substance, were they images and shadows of himself?

He turned to see if others saw them, or if he had conjured them to his private sight. But there was no-one to ask, for all were absorbed in their own agonies. Back to the darkened faces, changed and yet the same, he looked, and saw that they were dying. Each was speaking, long and low, neither seeming to hear the other. Whether they had objective life or were parts of himself, he knew the same spirit informed them that had lit and darkened the forms of Antonio and Sabrinus.

Next day they did indeed die and with others were buried at sea. But —

he told me — not only then but now at the moment of recounting — he felt they would return to him, or he to them.

His inquiries clarified nothing — they were two among a crowd of Lascar hands. He left the ship at her port of destination and stayed ashore for over a year, drifting from one occupation to another; but at length returned to the sea. He has not yet seen them again, Antonio and Sabrinus.

A darkness enclosed the whole story
though in the beginning
a serene, even, sourceless light
veiled the darkness.

Did they know one another?
The hammocks were slung
one alongside the other
but the two sailors each addressed darkness.

Was it Antonio and Sabrinus or his double shadow?
Were they his shadow and themselves?
Had their intensity a substance
out of his sight?

Darkness enclosed his story. He would be waiting
to see them again.

• RELATIVE FIGURES REAPPEAR

She, returned in the form of youth
black of hair and dress
curls deaf in a poem.

He, returned, sits as he would never sit
perched on a radiator, smoking,
balking sullenly at an obscure outrage.

Only she who still lives, not as then but in
the white hair of today, awkwardly
laughs, at a loss for right words.
Three familiar spirits present to me.

The lamb and the ram removed
from the packing case are neither
gentle nor potent, but gray dead
of having never lived, weightless
plaster forms. What comes

live (though a toy) out of the box
is a black fox. Is it a fox?

The dead girl rejoices. (But wait —
only now I remember she too is living
changed by time and inward fires.)
She takes the black animal I give her

64

in her arms, its sharp nose
poked at the long poem she is sunk in.

He is gone to another room angry
because the boy-child has seen
a diagram of the womb. Why?
Implacably laughing

(now I laugh too) but unsure
of my justice, I turn to assuage
a quick fear my black sister is prying

into my world, but the garnered
poems, stirring letters, dreams,
are undisturbed on the open desk.
She reads on and is dear to me.

• XOCHIPILLI

Xochipilli, god of spring
                            is sitting
on the earth floor, gazing
into a fire. In the fire
a serpent is preening, uncoiling.

"From thy dung
the red flowers," says the god.

By the hearth
bodies of hares and mice,
food for the snake.

"From thy bones
white flowers," says the god.

Rain dances many-footed
on the thatch. Raindrops
leap into the fire, the serpent hisses.

"From this music
seeds of the grass
that shall sing when the wind blows."
                    The god stirs the fire.

• THE QUARRY POOL

Between town and the
old house, an inn —
the Half-Way House.
So far one could ride, I remember,

the rest was an uphill walk,
a mountain lane with
steep banks and sweet
hedges, half walls of

gray rock. Looking
again at this looking-glass face
unaccountably changed in a week,
three weeks, a month,

I think without thinking of
Half-Way House. Is it
the thought that this far
I've driven at ease, as in a bus,

a country bus where one could talk to the driver?
Now on foot towards the village;
the dust clears, silence
draws in around one. I hear
the rustle and hum of the fields: alone.

67

It must be the sense
of essential solitude that chills me
looking into my eyes.
I should remember

the old house at the walk's ending,
a square place with a courtyard,
granaries, netted strawberry-beds,
a garden that was many

gardens, each one
a world hidden from the
next by leaves, enlaced trees,
fern-hairy walls, gilly-flowers.

I should see, making
a strange face at myself,
nothing to fear in the thought of
Half-Way House —

the place one got down
to walk —. What is
this shudder, this
dry mouth?

Think, please, of the quarry pool,
the garden's furthest
garden, of your childhood's
joy in its solitude.

• THE PARK

A garden of illusions!
Hidden by country trees, elm, oak,
wise thorn, and the tall green hedges of a maze,
the carpenters are preparing marvels!

But across the street the family
only glance toward the park gates,
stand clustered,
hesitant in their porch.

Already a ghost of fire
glides on the lake! In a mist
the flames of its body
pass shuddering over the dark ripples.

But they turn their heads
away, the tall people,
they talk and delay.

Waiting, I leap over
beds of glowing heart's-ease,
leaf-gold, fox-red, violet, deep
fur-brown, sailing high and slow

above them, descending
light and soft at their far borders.

69

But across the ice-crackling roadway
the house stands in midwinter daylight
and my friends neither in nor out of the house
still ignore the preparations of magic

the darkening of the garden
the flashes that may be summer lightning or
trials of illusion, the balconies
carved in a branchless towering oak.

Only the boy, my son, at last
ready, comes, and discovers joyfully
a man playing the horn
that is the true voice of the fire-ghost,

and believes in all wonders to come
in the park over-the-way,
country of open secrets where the elm
shelters the construction of gods
and true magic exceeds all design.

• ART
(After Gautier)

The best work is made
from hard, strong materials,
      obstinately precise —
the line of the poem, onyx, steel.

It's not a question of
false constraints — but
      to move well and get somewhere
wear shoes that fit.

To hell with easy rhythms —
sloppy mules that anyone can
      kick off or
step into.

Sculptor, don't bother with modeling
pliant clay; don't let
      a touch of your thumb
set your vision while it's still vague.

Pit yourself against granite,
hew basalt, carve hard ebony —
      intractable
guardians of contour.

Renew the power men had in Azerbaijan
to cast ethereal intensity in bronze
        and give it
force to endure any number of thousand years.

Painter, let be the 'nervous scratches' the
trick spontaneity; learn to see again,
        construct, break through
to 'the thrill of continuance with the appearance of all its changes,'[1]

towards that point where 'art becomes
a realization with which the urge to live
        collaborates as a mason.'[2] Use
'the mind's tongue, that works and tastes into the very rock heart.'[3]

Our lives flower and pass. Only robust
works of the imagination live in eternity,
        Tlaloc, Apollo,
dug out alive from dead cities.

And the austere coin
a tractor turns up in a
        building site
reveals an emperor.

[1] *Cezanne*
[2] *Jean Hélion*
[3] *Ruskin*

The gods die every day
but sovereign poems go on breathing
        in a counter-rhythm that mocks
the frenzy of weapons, their impudent power.

Incise, invent, file to poignance;
make your elusive dream
        seal itself
in the resistant mass of crude substance.

• TO THE SNAKE

Green Snake, when I hung you round my neck
and stroked your cold, pulsing throat
        as you hissed to me, glinting
arrowy gold scales, and I felt
        the weight of you on my shoulders,
and the whispering silver of your dryness
        sounded close at my ears —

Green Snake — I swore to my companions that certainly
        you were harmless! But truly
I had no certainty, and no hope, only desiring
        to hold you, for that joy,
                which left
a long wake of pleasure, as the leaves moved
and you faded into the pattern
of grass and shadows, and I returned
smiling and haunted, to a dark morning.